Love Poems
For Someone

James B Lyons

Spectrum Publications

First published in Australia in 2004
by Spectrum Publications Pty Ltd
PO Box 75, Richmond, Vic, 3121
Telephone: +61(3) 9 429 1404, Facsimile: +61(3) 9 428 9407
e-mail: spectrum@spectrumpublications.com.au
web: www.spectrumpublications.com.au

Copyright 2004 James B Lyons
All rights reserved.

No part of this publication may be reproduced
in any manner without prior
written permission of the publisher.

The Scripture quoted is from The Jerusalem Bible,
copyright 1966 by Darton, Longman & Todd Ltd and
Doubleday and Company Inc.

All photographs are by the Author.
Design: Kelly Drinkwater
Typesetting by Spectrum Publications
Typeface: Goudy Old Style
ISBN 0 86786 358 7

Gratefully dedicated to
Paul and Sue
and their house by the sea
where love is always at home.

Reflections on 1 Corinthians 13

Love is always patient and kind;
it is never jealous
love is never boastful or conceited;
it is never rude or selfish;
it does not take offence, and is not resentful.
Love takes no pleasure in other people's sins
but delights in the truth;
it is always ready to excuse, to trust, to hope,
and to endure whatever comes.
Love does not come to an end.

1 Corinthians 13: 4-8 (JB)

Table of Contents

Introduction	viii
Love is Always Patient	1
Love is Always Kind	5
Love is Never Jealous	9
Love is Never Boastful or Conceited	13
Love is Never Rude or Selfish	17
Love Does Not Take Offence	21
Love is Not Resentful	25
Love Takes No Pleasure in Other People's Sins	29
Love Delights in the Truth	33
Love is Always Ready to Excuse and to Trust	37
Love Hopes	41
Love is Always Ready to Endure Whatever Comes	45
Love Does Not Come to an End	49
Love Speaks - for Maggie and Mark	53
Love is the Gift	55

Introduction

The most popular choice for a scripture reading in a wedding liturgy is the section from St Paul's letter to the Corinthians in which he defines love. However, a couple I was once working with did not choose it and told me why. "It's a beautiful reading but there's too much in it. The ideals are great but they overwhelm us." The comment started me wondering about this beautiful reading, attractive to such a large number of couples yet, for some, quite off-putting.

Paul's multi-faceted definition of love, conjures up many experiences in relationships. We can easily say Yes to them all, for that's exactly the way we would like to live. But as we ponder these ideals they can, quite quickly, overwhelm.

Grouped together, the descriptions of love make a fine tapestry, woven with disarming charm. Their immediate attraction can cloud the reality that love can only be all these things through effort and failure, understanding and forgiveness, and open, honest channels of communication.

I have no wish to discourage couples from including this scripture in their marriage celebration, or indeed its use in any liturgy. Quite the opposite. It is the Word of God that speaks in the scriptures; a Word that brings the gift of love we find uniquely in Jesus Christ. I offer these pages as a reflection on this Word, in the hope that the "Love is always" passage will be seen for what it really is - a vast reservoir of insights into the very nature of God, who is Love. [1John, 4:8]

In sharing my own experiences as a pastor, a friend and a person, bound up in the pursuit of love, I gratefully acknowledge my indebtedness to those who have loved my into life. Their patience, kindness, compassion, trust, forgiveness, honesty, and, above all, their presence, have opened doors to the treasury of love.

My parents were my first teachers in faith and love. Others have continued their artistry. Our own loving is shaped by those who love us.

May this book bring a deeper appreciation of the power that is love and the gift that is Jesus. May it not overwhelm but greatly encourage.

Love is always.

James B Lyons

Love is Always Patient

During my years with Catholic Communications I was concerned to encourage television and radio programmes that would bring out aspects of faith in the ordinariness of people's lives. The 30 seconds "spots" in which a Christian message came out of an everyday experience was particularly appealing. It not only matched the commercial image of the electronic media, its brevity made the message more memorable.

One such "tele-spot" opened with an elderly woman sitting by her window. Her phone started to ring. She got up and reached for her walking frame, beginning a slow journey across the room to get the call. This took about 20 seconds of the programme and a first time viewer's reaction was invariably, "She's not going to make it before the phone stops ringing!" But she does make it. She lifts the receiver to her ear and her face lights up as she hears her granddaughter's voice, "Hi grandma!" The scene freezes and a caption appears: LOVE WAITS.

Waiting is not an easy position in a world of movement and fast paced activity. In an "instant" age delays are intolerable. Some people won't even stand in a queue but would rather find something else to do and come back later. Waiting is so negative! And very unproductive!

Patience is waiting. It waits and it hopes. Patience believes in the value of waiting, knowing that not everyone can move at the same pace, or see things from the same perspective. Patience understands waiting as an essential ingredient to change and growth. Patience says, "I can wait for you. You are worth waiting for."

You are so patient with me.
I know the way -
Or so I tell myself
And you let me go
But not alone.

    For you know that soon
    I'll need to start again
    Retrace my steps
    Damaged pride much heavier
    Than any bags I carry.

        It's then you touch my arm
        And I turn to meet your eyes
        Loving me beyond my foolishness
        Cradling my hurt
        In their deep pool of mercy.

        You are so patient with me.

            Waiting out my failures
            Nurturing the love seeds in my heart
            Calling them to life
            In the time you have given me
            Until we reach home.

Love is Always Kind

"Kind words are the music of the world. They have a power which seems to be beyond natural causes, as though they were some angel's song which had lost its way and come to earth."
[Frederick William Faber, 1814-1863]

The above quote seems to suggest that "kind words" are alien visitors that somehow found their way to earth. Its their power that signals they are not of us. Kindness has a way of transforming what it touches. Melting frozen hearts, removing blind spots, reconciling differences, disarming prejudice - these are some of the results of kindness. Yet surely as much the stuff of this world as revenge and "user pays" and giving as good as you get!

How we warm to kindness. And how kindness warms. A word of thanks or sympathy or asking if you need a hand. A word that is said with the eyes or with a hand on your arm. A word disguised as a basket of freshly made scones. A word you hear in the smile of your friend or in the roughly picked flower held up to you by your child, or grandchild.

If kind words "have a power which seem to be beyond natural causes", perhaps it is because love is of the spirit and tugs us to move beyond what is simply natural.

The kindness in love tells me I'm not alone. Whether it's me reaching out to help someone, or others touching me with their "wanting to help", kindness brings a companionship that lifts burdens and encourages hope.

If our expression "You're an angel!" echoes the seeming "unworldly" nature of kindness, it might equally identify an inner reality which kindness helps reveal.

Love is kind
Because
Love takes time
And
Takes the time

    To see
    To hear
    To understand

And is there
Present

    To a need
    To a fear
    To a moment of joy

Kindness in love
Moves close
And touches
It brings a word
And in the word
Life

Love is Never Jealous

If you share secretly in the joy of someone you envy, you will be freed from your jealousy; and you will also be freed from your jealousy if you keep silent about the person you envy.
                    Seventh Century Monk (Libya)

In jealousy there is more self-love than love.
                    Seventeenth Century Writer (France)

The biblical story commonly known as "The Prodigal Son" has a large helping of jealousy in it.

The younger son asks for, and gets, his share of the family inheritance and leaves home. We are not told what prompted his request or his departure. Perhaps he just wanted to see the world. Or, perhaps, he saw little chance for his own advancement with an older brother to contend with. He was certainly self-centred. The good of the family - which was threatened by the breaking up of the estate - was not his primary concern.

His return uncovers jealous resentment in the older brother.

He refuses to join the welcome home party. His anger blocks his forgiveness. The story ends with the brothers still unreconciled. Their envy of one another is mutually destructive. (cf Luke, 15: 11-32)

Love cannot be found in jealousy because love seeks the other, not what the other has. Love admires the gift in the other person, seeing how the gift enhances, beautifies, adorns the life of that person. Love does not want the gift for itself, for love knows that the gift would not have the same effect in anyone else.

When you choose a gift for a friend you choose something you feel the friend will like. You choose it to match personality, or to add to or complement a favourite item, such as music or books or paintings. Rarely would you select an identical gift for two separate friends. Everyone is different, unique.

Love is never jealous because love understands this uniqueness.

> There she goes again. Sounding
> off about some topic
> so knowing
> so confident.
>
> And yes, if I am honest, I
> admit it's not pretence. She
> really knows
> what she's talking about.

But I can't stand the
sound or sight of her.

> Jealousy.
> My twisted way of loving.
> Admiring the gifts in others
> yet hating them because
> they are not my own.
>
> > Jealousy.
> > The meal of my hunger for acceptance.
> > But never satisfying. Instead
> > eating away my self esteem
> > poisoning my life.
>
> The gifts in others can
> never be mine apart
> from those who have them.
> When we accept each other
> our gifts are shared.
> When we let go of jealousy
> love smiles and lives grow.

Love is Never Boastful or Conceited

Morrie Schwartz was dying. His disease would gradually rob him of all movement. Logically he would slowly suffocate as his lungs became incapable of working. Once a week Mitch Albom visited his former sociology professor and found, that far from limiting his interest in life, Morrie's illness gave him a platform from which to share wonderful, if challenging, insights.

"Tuesdays With Morrie" is Mitch Albom's tribute to his mentor. Its recurring theme is Morrie's claim that "when you learn how to die you learn to live" and his conviction that love is the only winner in life's tensions and conflicts. He told Mitch his disease had taught him that "the most important thing in life is to learn how to give out love, and to let it come in".

Boasting and conceit fly in the face of that insight because they are concerned with having rather than giving: "Look what I've got!" "Look how clever I am!" "Don't you wish you were like me?" "Aren't you jealous?"

The boastful and conceited invite envy. There is no question of sharing what they have, or giving it away, only displaying it, holding it up to tease and tempt, to tantalize and torment.

The boastful and conceited want to hang on to their possessions, their position, their influence, their power, at all costs. They are not people who let go easily.

Morrie Schwartz would say that what such people really want is to be noticed and to be wanted for themselves - just like everyone else. But they end up keeping people out. Love cannot penetrate barriers locked against giving.

Look what I've got!
Can't you tell how successful
I am just by looking
At me?

See how clever I am!
Don't you know it takes skill
To get to be clever
Like me?

Yes I see what you've got
It's all gift
Didn't you know?
Where's the skill in that?

Can you share it?
Can you pass it on?
Can you let it go?
There's skill in that.

Love is Never Rude or Selfish

Lewis Carroll, of Alice and Wonderland fame, wrote "One of the deepest secrets of life is that all that is really worth doing is what we do for others."

Through Alice he illustrates that secret in her adventures and especially in the characters she meet along the way. Rudeness and selfishness are like paving stones threatening to trip Alice, so often alarmed by attitudes that are "anything but nice."

"No room! No room!" cry the March Hare and the Hatter when Alice approaches their tea table. But of course there is plenty of room. Later she accepts their offer of wine only to be told "There isn't any".

"Your hair wants cutting," says the Hatter. That is quite enough for Alice and she bursts out with "You should learn not to make personal remarks. It's very rude."

"Off with his head" is the Queen's way of settling all difficulties. And the Rabbit frightens Alice with his demanding ways.

But Alice wins through, helping others as she tries to understand the maze that traps her. She saves a group of "curious creatures" from drowning in the Pool of Tears and hides the gardeners when the Queen would have their heads. Even the Tea Party, at first spiced with rudeness, becomes a friendly affair.

Rudeness shouts out my presence and tells the world how important I think I am. It is my weapon of intrusion that makes sure people know I'm around.

I make a smart comment at the expense of someone else's embarrassment. I point out a fault, like the wrong use of a word in a conversation, or the wearing of an out-of-fashion or wrong-occasion garment. People laugh. I'm noticed. But someone is hurt. My rudeness is costly company.

Rudeness shows up selfishness. It takes no account of any feelings except my own. Rudeness is insensitive. It is hungry for attention and looks for the biggest slice of the action whether invited or not. It pushes its way to the front without thinking of consequences.

The rude and the selfish are partners in a dance that steps its way across the lives of other people, hurting, annoying, alienating - and in the end destroying any chance of linking up in friendship or community.

Love cannot be rude or selfish because love does not think of itself ahead of other people. Love looks for the good, not bothered by the fault. Love's presence brings people closer; it doesn't drive them away. Love comes to serve, not to be served.

You who came to serve
and not to be served
who took the path
that led to others and
paid the price of caring

help me serve with you.

        You who left your rest
        to calm the storm in hearts
        too full of fear
        to care or bear the scourge
        of doubts or needful cries

        lead me from my rest.

                You who wept for company
                when sleep dismissed your friends
                and darkness dripped
                despair and stole your peace
                and kissed you in betrayal

                keep me by your side.

Love Does Not Take Offence

How brittle we are. How easily hurt. Like china cups we need to be handled with great care. Or so we tell ourselves.

It's so easy to take offence, to feel slighted or put down. Someone misinterprets a gesture or comment you make and immediately you conclude they don't like you or are out to make you look foolish. You work hard to tidy the house, to present yourself well for an occasion, to put yourself out for someone, and no one notices or says how well you've done. You withdraw into yourself, feeling unappreciated, terribly hurt.

Most people never know when they've offended someone. That's because most offences are self-inflicted. You "take offence" at something said or done or omitted because it clashes with your expectations and has little or nothing to do with the other person's feelings or motivation.

Love says let go of some of your sensitivity. You are not as brittle as you think. You can take harder knocks than those that come with not being noticed. Love does not take offence because it's busy noticing and appreciating what others are contributing to life. Love has more to do than feel sorry for itself. Among other things, it has to make sure that nothing in its own actions ever gives offence.

Love does not take offence because love understands. Love understands the weakness, the insecurity, the lack of self-esteem, and all the many other things that can lead to giving offence.

Love does not take offence because love is compassionate. Love walks in the sandals of the other person and so feels the same rough ground, and trips and stumbles along the same way.

Love does not take offence because love forgives.

It was such a silly thing
I don't know why I let it bother me
But the words were out before I could check myself
And now a friend is hurt.

    How stupid I was how selfish
    So what if I felt offended
    It was really no big deal and in the end a mistake
    On my part.

So quick to cut and wound
The healing so uncertain
A friendship torn and shredded with a word
Now a chasm lies between us.

    I hurt you my friend
    My sorrow seeks forgiveness
    In this giving you can help me make the change
    That love might be renewed.

Love is Not Resentful

nother word for resentful is aggrieved. That tells me that feelings of resentment have more than a trace of grief in them. Grieving is mourning, aching over some loss, sorrowing for hurt you've experienced, or for having to let go of a person or possession greatly loved.

Resentfulness is grief that has become embittered. It strikes out at the cause of the grief, harbouring a grudge, refusing to let go of the hurt with the same intensity that once clung to what is no longer available.

Some years ago, the families of two Auckland boys killed by a car greeted the accused driver with open arms and forgiveness. Their action was headline news because it was so unexpected. More than that, the boys were Samoan and the driver a Tongan. But instead of inflaming racial tension the two communities held a service of reconciliation.

In 1995, 50 years after the conclusion of the Second World War, many countries celebrated with wreath laying ceremonies at war memorials. The occasion gave rise to some anti-Japanese sentiment as war veterans recalled atrocities and said they could neither "forgive nor forget" what they had seen happen to their comrades.

Others said that continuing hatred would achieve nothing, except to hurt those who did the hating.

Learning that love is not resentful is learning to let go of hurt, loosening your grip on the deep down anger that has coloured, or rather discoloured, your life. This will probably involve the healing of memories, facing and resolving those images that were formed from past, hurtful experiences.

Healing memories is not the same as forgetting them. They stay with us because they are part of who we are. But the healing process enables them to find a different place in your life. Once healed, memories that earlier hurt and scarred with resentment, let us move on. We're different because of them. Self-knowledge strengthens; self-awareness improves. Maturity and growth occur.

And the lesson learned? Love is not and can never be resentful.

I caught you from the corner of my eye
A speck. A hint of your approach
A tell-tale signal that announced you
And I froze.

Suddenly
You were in front of me
The words of long ago
That seared and scarred my life
were tumbling towards me
And there was no escape.

The now about me
Told me this was of the past
But the memory was so real
And I knew my resentfulness
Had not abated
Just hidden and waited.

Sometimes we hurt each other
That happens in life
But to hold the hurt
To nurse it, even to nourish it
Is to harm beyond the meaning of the word
No freedom to be found there
And no way to love.

Love Takes No Pleasure in Other People's Sins

Gossip, hearsay, innuendo.

Phrases like "Did you know...?" or "You don't mean...?" Drivers and passengers "rubber-necking" as they pass an accident, slowing and even blocking traffic. Sightseers hindering rescue teams after a landslide engulfs holiday homes, or blocking access to fire crews trying to reach a blazing house...

We are fascinated by the misfortune that happens to others and the troubles that other people get into. Especially the rich and famous. In 1997, American sport star O.J. Simpson was tried for the murder of his wife. The trial was televised live and became a "box office hit" with a global audience of millions. It created a world wide market in memorabilia from T-shirts to bumper stickers.

There are always people ready to exploit a situation for personal gain, and our insatiable appetite for the secrets in people's lives plays right into their hands.

The saying, "There but for the grace of God go I!" is a reminder that circumstances, social environment, opportunities and "the roll of a dice" can make all the difference between your involvement in an accident or someone else's; a failure on your part or someone else's; you taking a deliberate decision to do something you know to be wrong, and someone else's non involvement.

Love takes no pleasure in either the awful things that happen to people or the awful things that people do.

Love understands the vulnerability of every person and the interconnectedness of everyone. What happens to one happens to all. Love rejoices in helping to heal, not tearing down; in forgiving, not condemning.

How close I came to messing things up.

That moment of indecision
now that I can look back on it
was just the decision I needed.

Imagine if I'd gone ahead.
The hurt the heartbreak
yours and mine.

And the others so quick to pounce
to point the finger to gloat.

I've done it myself.
"Come back for the matinee!"
And I've laughed because
it wasn't my pain on show.

But now I understand

Laugh not judge not.
Love the sinner not the sin.
Own the pain, support it, heal it.

There with the grace of God go I.

Love Delights in the Truth

"Truth. What is truth?" Pilate's question to Jesus. 2000 years ago has not lost its impact. Or its importance. Or its significance. In all our relationships.

"Truth is what I say is true," screams the dictator. "Truth is whatever is true for you," comforts the counsellor. And our courts still expect "the truth, the whole truth and nothing but the truth." What is truth?

The dictionary tells us simply that truth is the "Quality or state of being true or truthful" and defines "True" as whatever is "In accordance with fact or reality".

Jesus said, "I am the truth!" What are we to make of that?

Like beauty, truth is seen more than touched, instinctively recognised and less objectively known. A parent knows when a child is not telling the truth, even though a bystander might be happy to accept what the child says. Close friends find it impossible to hide the truth from one another. Truth can show itself in our eyes; it has a way of being heard through what we do not say; it can come to meet us like someone we haven't seen for a long time, catching us off guard. Remember the old adage, "Truth will out!"

Love delights in the truth as new born lambs leap and bounce with the excitement of life.

Love smiles and nods approvingly when there is no deceit, when people trust each other enough to speak openly, honestly.

Love delights when truth does not have to be camouflaged or compromised, but can stand naked in the light without shame.

Love and Truth
The perfect match
A delightful couple
Delighting to be in each other's company
Made for each other
Loving and truthful
Truthful and loving
Holding hands and walking into life
Creating life
And a home

Love is Always Ready to Excuse and to Trust

The years of my life and the days of my years have taught me about myself. They have shown up my mistakes even when I was sure they were well hidden. They have also pointed out possibilities and opportunities I side-stepped or avoided. And I see, in the days and years that have been, steps taken and retraced, opinions firmly held and later changed, and a faith sometimes strong and sometimes very fragile.

But most of my years and days have taught me trust - the quality of love that holds on and doesn't give up, that instinctively knows that pain will pass, sorrow will melt, disappointment will be transformed by a new vision.

Trust tells me that life begins anew with each new day, and if night seems to shut down life it is only in order to renew life and to celebrate it with the freshness of dawn.

When you trust it is easy to excuse. Trust has a way of helping you to accept, and sometimes even to explain, limitations. Trust appreciates that differences don't necessarily signal confrontation or dishonesty. Trust makes room, allows time, and never expects perfection.

I admit to times when I thought I could never trust again. When help given has been abused, when promises have been broken or - as on at least one occasion - when going guarantor for someone has caused me great embarrassment. Surely there must be a limit!

But then I hear Jesus responding to Peter's question about forgiveness. "How many times ...?" (Matthew 18:21-22) and I know he'd give the same answer if the question was, "How many times do I excuse and trust?"

Only love makes excusing and trusting possible, because only love - being without self-interest - is not threatened by failure however inexcusable or blameworthy it may appear.

sand and sea
sea and sand
an ocean of interdependence
and total acceptance
one providing the base
and the boundary
the other the covering
the adornment
both teem with life
and live in mutual trust
coming into each other's life
just far enough
just far enough.

                        sand and sea
                        sea and sand
                        neither one
                        too big
                        for the other or
                        too small
                        you teach me
                        about relationships
                        how to hold
                        in trust
                        and to last
                        in love
                        in love.

Love Hopes

> *Hope springs eternal in the human breast.*
> Alexander Pope

lthough primarily a lesson about mercy, the Parable of the Prodigal Son [Luke 15] can help with the problem of jealousy through the character of the elder brother. The errant son found forgiveness awaited him at home, but also the hardened and embittered heart of his elder brother.

Another aspect of this great parable is its emphasis on hope.

In the story, the father agrees to his son's request that he be given his share of the family fortune and be allowed to leave home. There is no further reference to the father until the son, disillusioned and discarded, makes his decision to return home. Then we read,

While he was still a long way off, his father saw him and was moved with pity. He ran to the boy, clasped him in his arms and kissed him. [verse 20]

A child may leave home but not the parent's heart.

The father saw the son while he was still a long way off. That tells us he never gave up on his boy. Hope kept him in sight. Love brought him home.

Parents agonise over their children, whose need to be independent comes mostly before they understand that they must also be interdependent. The resulting rebellion can be heartbreaking for those whose love has given and nourished the lives of those now in turmoil.

Parents have told me of the pain of their powerlessness as their teenage son or daughter defies their authority, refuses to identify with the family, demands independence, spurns their trust, and/or while still clearly ill-equipped emotionally or materially, breaks away from the home environment.

At such times, love hopes.

Love hopes that the loved one will be alright. Love hopes that the relationship will not be permanently broken. Love hopes that, despite all appearances to the contrary, the loved one will grow, find happiness, and one day return. And then, love hopes there will be no judgement, no blaming, but only a warm welcoming embrace.

Love hopes
always believing the best
and trusting the goodness
that is the God-part
in everyone.

        Love hopes
        in a change of heart
        and a melting
        of the ice-cold bitterness
        that clamps and cramps resolve.

Love hopes
that tears will cleanse
and life will flourish
that scars will heal
and that hands will reach and hold.

        Love hopes
        for joy in friendship
        and peace in pardon
        for reunion
        and time to say I love you.

Love is Always Ready to Endure Whatever Comes

I promise to be true to you in good times and in bad, in sickness and in health. I will love you and honour you all the days of my life.

Marriage Vows

It is the readiness of love to endure that is celebrated here. Love will crash at the first test if it hasn't readied itself to endure whatever comes.

This quality of love is probably best alluded to in the marriage vows. They centre on a promise to be in the life of the loved one no matter what. If you are sick I will be there for you; if you're troubled I'll support you; whatever times we find ourselves in - good, bad or indifferent - we'll work through each day together; whatever comes to disturb or threaten or challenge, we'll outlast it!

To be ready to endure implies that you have thought and prayed about numerous possibilities. An accident may take away the ability to work; a redundancy may equally destroy your employment options. Dreams you had dreamed together may prove too idealistic; habits you hoped might change may simply deepen; friends you relied on may disappear; temptations may prove too strong.

In our disposable culture, where nothing is made or meant to last, endurance is a strange concept. When a household appliance breaks or fails it's usually cheaper to buy a new one than to pay for repairs. When something goes wrong in a marriage or friendship we risk applying the same criteria.

Endurance enables us to continue to value what is most dear to us even though, for a time, it may lose its appeal or seem beyond reach.

Yet love is not inactive, lying in a state of readiness with nothing to do except wait for something to endure. Love has spoken its choice and now, through thick and thin, wants to maintain course.

The two parties in a relationship have to work together. Love can neither live nor grow in a vacuum. It takes the We in the relationship seriously. Mutual respect, acceptance of differences, and a willingness to bend a little, accommodate and make allowances, are all part of the mix that blend a perfect response when endurance is called for.

He never saw it coming!
It was a comment meant to help
to soften the shock
of discovering the note
on the table
among the plates from yesterday
and yesterday.

      But it was true of both of them.
      They never saw anything coming
      so there was no preparation
      no readiness
      and therefore not much talking
      or anything else that might
      let them take trouble in their stride.

            Love had always been so easy.
            So easy in fact
            they never really valued it
            or saw its value
            or understood its cost.
            It takes a lot for love to be ready
            to endure whatever comes.

Love Does Not Come to an End

Gail was 21 when she married Dennis.
I had the privilege of witnessing their marriage, joining their hands as they promised "to love and honour" each other for the rest of their lives. 26 years later we were together again. This time in a hospice room. Gail had battled for over a year with cancer and death was now just a few hours away.

Sadness not joy this time. But another privileged moment.

Gail could no longer speak but her eyes flickered in response as Dennis spoke his love one more time. His words turned the pages of their 26 years and he told, bravely and gently, of the shared laughter and sorrow that had stitched them together into a book of life. Gail's busy presence in the home, her generous care of the children, her determination, her no nonsense approach to problem solving, her faithfulness and her loveliness as mother, wife and woman.

After a while Dennis had no more words, or no more voice to utter them. It was then, in their hand-held silence that they truly spoke, and I understood the meaning of "A man will leave his father and mother and be joined to his wife, and the two will become one."

I left them there. Silent and together as one. The love gift they had made to each other 26 years earlier, had been gratefully received, proudly displayed, and always respected.

As they let each other go in the separation of death there was no awkwardness, no signs of despair. They believed in their love. It might pierce them with sadness, but it would also heal. And keep healing. Until death was no more.

You are a bird in flight
Soaring, turning, climbing
Shimmering in reflected light
And reflecting light
In loving waves of moving wings
That speak an endless silence.

You are a bird in flight
Confident and distant
Your confidence brimming through
The network of all that supports you
Your distance held close in sight
Through the window of memory.

You are a bird in flight
Not fleeing but leading
Always hoping and expecting hope
Moving with grateful purpose
Just beyond my reach
An image of graceful freedom
Calling me on...

Love Speaks - for Maggie and Mark

We spoke not nearly long enough
to fill the time since our last conversation
but we spoke of love
your love for one another
and that told me all was well
with my friend of far off days.

You have grown with love
and now that love is sealed
in a marriage of lives
becoming one in heart and hope
gifting your best to each other
with tomorrow in your joined hands.

Come let us pray the blessing of love
for the two of you now truly one
be blessed with life to give and receive
with hearts to warm and care
with time to share and time to heal
and with shelter enough for all.

God be with you, Maggie and Mark

Love is the Gift

You asked me what my gift was
The day we talked of gifts
And giftedness

And I said, Words

Or rather, my love of words.

Love is the gift.

The desire, the delight and
The joy to hold a word
And free it into life.

To feel its sudden swiftness
Sparkling, surprising
In its lightness and its strength.

Touching where no hand can reach
Creating a mood
Changing a world

Climbing in and out of lives

Sometimes resting
Sometimes nesting, and
Sometimes

Like Noah's dove
Finding dry land
And a new home.

If I have the eloquence of men or of angels,
but speak without love,
I am simply a gong booming or a cymbal clashing.
If I have the gift of prophecy,
understanding all the mysteries there are,
and knowing everything,
and if I have faith in all its fullness,
to move mountains, but without love,
then I am nothing at all.
If I give away all that I possess, piece by piece,
and if I even let them take my body to burn it,
but am without love,
it will do me no good whatever.

Love is always patient and kind;
it is never jealous;
love is never boastful or conceited;
it is never rude or selfish;
it does not take offence,
and is not resentful.
Love takes no pleasure in other people's sins
but delights in the truth;
it is always ready to excuse, to trust, to hope,
and to endure whatever comes.

Love does not come to an end.
But if there are gifts of prophecy
the time will come when they must fail;
or the gift of languages, it will not
continue forever...

There are three things that last:
faith, hope and love;
and the greatest of these is love.
(1 Cor.13: 1-8; 13)

Acknowledgements

I am grateful to the many people who have welcomed me into their lives and have accompanied me with their love. Their stories of loving and hurting and healing are the soil that sheltered and nourished the seed that has become this book.. The wisdom and honesty of those who critiqued the work have also contributed to the publication of LOVE IS ALWAYS. My sincere thanks to all.

Whoever does not love does not know God, because God is love.

1 John 4:8